# Little

# RIDDLERS

## North London

Edited By Daisy Job

First published in Great Britain in 2018 by:

YoungWriters

Young Writers
Remus House
Coltsfoot Drive
Peterborough
PE2 9BF
Telephone: 01733 890066
Website: www.youngwriters.co.uk

SB ISBN 978-1-78896-499-9
Printed and bound in the UK by BookPrintingUK
Website: www.bookprintinguk.com
YB0363Z

# FOREWORD

Dear Reader,

Are you ready to get your thinking caps on to puzzle your way through this wonderful collection?

Young Writers' Little Riddlers competition set out to encourage young writers to create their own riddles. Their answers could be whatever or whoever their imaginations desired; from people to places, animals to objects, food to seasons. Riddles are a great way to further the children's use of poetic expression, including onomatopoeia and similes, as well as encourage them to 'think outside the box' by providing clues without giving the answer away immediately.

All of us here at Young Writers believe in the importance of inspiring young children to produce creative writing, including poetry, and we feel that seeing their own riddles in print will keep that creative spirit burning brightly and proudly.

We hope you enjoy riddling your way through this book as much as we enjoyed reading all the entries.

# CONTENTS

## Rimon Jewish Primary School, Golders Green

| | |
|---|---|
| Isabella Clifford (6) | 63 |
| Zac Reuben (7) | 64 |
| Max Silverman (6) | 65 |
| Emilie Vertes (7) | 66 |
| Sammy Belnikoff (7) | 67 |
| Zeph Quint (6) | 68 |
| Eliana Barasi (7) | 69 |
| Mylee Victoria White (7) | 70 |
| Julia Movshovitz (6) | 71 |
| Lila Barasi (5) | 72 |
| Lily Greenfeld (6) | 73 |

## St James CE Primary School, Northampton

| | |
|---|---|
| Candre Chukwuemeka (7) | 74 |
| Abbie Radu (7) | 75 |

## St Mark's CE Primary School, Islington

| | |
|---|---|
| Darwin Kafka (7) | 76 |
| Amy Bala (7) | 77 |
| Joel Tesfamariam (7) | 78 |
| Joshua Daynes (6) | 79 |
| Inka Druszcz (7) | 80 |
| Tia Kallaste Akesen (6) | 81 |
| Ruby Parkhurst (6) | 82 |
| Layla Cole (7) | 83 |
| Poppy Haigh (7) | 84 |
| Yerim Baek (6) | 85 |
| Grace (7) | 86 |
| Yohana Yonata (5) | 87 |
| Nahom Yonata (7) | 88 |
| Cerys Rosel Miller (5) | 89 |
| Olive Boyd (5) | 90 |
| Malik Adam (6) | 91 |
| Mae English (5) | 92 |
| Alistair Turner (6) | 93 |
| Alicia Chin (5) | 94 |
| George Pipinka (6) | 95 |

| | |
|---|---|
| Shiloh Daley (5) | 96 |

## St Martin's School, Mill Hill

| | |
|---|---|
| Faith Leslie Smith (7) | 97 |
| Jin Kobayashi (6) | 98 |
| Bami Disu (6) | 99 |
| Michael Burgess (7) | 100 |
| Dylan Attar (7) | 101 |
| Max Ng (7) | 102 |
| Peter De Souza-Feighoney (6) | 103 |
| Alan Jalal (6) | 104 |

## Starks Field Primary School, Edmonton

| | |
|---|---|
| Emilio Mataj (7) | 105 |
| Ruby May Penn (6) | 106 |
| Halima Said (6) | 107 |
| Stefano Brusa (6) | 108 |
| Ellie Louise Richards (7) | 109 |
| Ameera Haque (7) | 110 |
| Jeremiah Chinonso Nwoke (6) | 111 |
| Aisling Dorcas Adejori (6) | 112 |
| Lily-Rose Cruickshank (7) | 113 |
| Gabriela Ivaylova Ivanova (7) | 114 |
| Christian Kardzhaliyski (7) | 115 |
| Mehnaz Alam (7) | 116 |
| Ediz Jeysan Ibrahim (7) | 117 |

## The Willow Primary School, Tottenham

| | |
|---|---|
| Abigail Jenny Ochan (7) | 118 |
| Renaé Beckford (7) | 119 |
| Abdulrahman Rage (7) | 120 |
| Solomon Goddard-Banks (6) | 121 |
| Natasha Anakaye Stevens (7) | 122 |
| Luis Ciku (7) | 123 |
| Ilhan Musah (7) | 124 |
| Ike Lemeh (7) | 125 |
| Nadirah Nasir (7) | 126 |
| Mert Tintas (6) | 127 |
| Prince Auguste (6) | 128 |

Jayden Taylor-Macauley (6)	129
Patrick Mpanumpanu (7)	130

## UCS Pre-Prep, London

Chukwuma Okongwu (5)	131
Sammy Kohansky (6)	132
Theo Postgate (5)	133
Freddie Harris (6)	134
Gabriel Susskind (6)	135
William Lacey (6)	136
Leah Livingstone (6)	137
Toby Allen (6)	138
Zac Collis (6)	139
Feyi Animashaun (6)	140
Max Tager (5)	141
Jacob Lee (5)	142
Adrian Bucher (5)	143
Enitan Ajeigbe (6)	144
Eric Wang (6)	145
Kabir Jai Bordoloi (5)	146
Ethan Shaw (5)	147
Sacha Livingstone (6)	148
Leo San (6)	149
Emily Pratt (5)	150
Even Chaitowitz (6)	151
Baer Bolton Smith (5)	152
Avyan Kapur (5)	153
Sasha Steele (5)	154
Reuben Jerman-Lipus (5)	155
Amit Kumar (6)	156
Max San (6)	157
Lily Grace Nyman (6)	158
Alfie Boujo (5)	159

## Wessex Gardens Primary School, Golders Green

Marie Allali (7)	160
Hassan Alaa (6)	161
Kinjal Rawat (7)	162
Ilhan Coskum (6)	163
Ali Aldahhan (6)	164

# THE POEMS

# What Are We?

A fish-lover.
A milk-drinker.
A lap-sitter.
A quiet purrer.
A bird-killer.
A water-hater.
A back-archer.
A bad biter.
A sleek sprinter.

A loud barker.
A keen licker.
A born discoverer.
A happy runner.
A fast eater.

What are we?

Answer: A cat and a dog.

## Elsie Armistead-Knowles (6)
Bruce Grove Primary School, Tottenham

# What Are We?

A milk-drinker.
A great chaser.
A food-lover.
A poo-maker.
A perfect runner.
A great scratcher.
A loud purrer.
A good helper.
A great walker.

A noisy barker.
A loud snorer.
A food-eater.
A super licker.
A poo-maker.
A bone-digger.
A super runner.
A perfect sniffer.

What are we?

Answer: A cat and a dog.

## Georgina Bonado Mendoza (6)
Bruce Grove Primary School, Tottenham

# What Am I?

A licker.
Beautiful fur.
A bad scratcher.
Warm hair.
A terrible biter.
A fast runner.
A little hider.
A long jumper.
A big pouncer.
A poo-maker.
A good eater.
A good drinker.
A people-liker.
A nice player.
What am I?

Answer: A cat.

## Diego Gonzalez-Bras (6)
Bruce Grove Primary School, Tottenham

# What Am I?

A loud barker.
A keen licker.
A noisy snorer.
A super sniffer.
A food-lover.
A good digger.
A great barker.
A soft eater.
A great sleeper.
A good runner.
A great pooer.
What am I?

Answer: Stella's dog.

## Stella Ramrakha (6)
Bruce Grove Primary School, Tottenham

# Who Am I?

A great hitter.
A perfect snorer.
A good private hire-driver.
A great shouter.
A good eater.
A great helper.
A good teacher.
A good drinker.
A perfect teller.
A great breather.
Who am I?

Answer: My dad.

## Mohammad Shaikhzada (6)
Bruce Grove Primary School, Tottenham

# What Am I?

A good fighter.
A good eater.
A fast mover.
A good pouncer.
Makes loud noises.
A fast runner.
A good runner.
A fast pouncer.
A good mover.
A food-lover.
A good walker.
What am I?

Answer: A tiger.

## Omar Nahas (7)
Bruce Grove Primary School, Tottenham

# What Am I?

A great fighter.
An awesome biter.
A cool pouncer.
A bad killer.
A soft tail.
A fast runner.
A food-lover.
A good mover.
A good walker.
A good eater.
A stripy tail.
What am I?

Answer: A cheetah.

## Zakaria Joyub (7)
Bruce Grove Primary School, Tottenham

# What Am I?

A dangerous fighter.
A perfect sniffer.
A good snorer.
An awful animal.
A bad barker.
A fast runner.
A generous biter.
An enormous and fluffy one.
What am I?

Answer: A dog.

**Ionut Adrian Bri (6)**
Bruce Grove Primary School, Tottenham

# What Am I?

A world-class kicker.
A stronger player.
A cool passer.
A good tackler.
A fierce attacker.
A fast runner.
A bad pusher.
A goal-scorer.
What am I?

Answer: A footballer.

## Yasin Hussain (7)
Bruce Grove Primary School, Tottenham

# What Am I?

A cat-hater.
A super sniffer.
A bone-lover.
A loud barker.
A poo-maker.
A sleepyhead.
A lap-sitter.
A cute animal.
A furry friend.
What am I?

*Answer: A dog.*

## Kai Pierre-Reid (7)
Bruce Grove Primary School, Tottenham

# Water Fun

I can be rectangular, I can be square.
There's lots of water in there.
Use your goggles to see underwater
And have fun with your son or daughter.
Lots of fun for young and old,
Let's hope the water is not too cold.
You can splash your daddy in the face,
You can even have a race!
We go there every Sunday
Because it's our favourite fun day.
Jumping in gets you wet
And your towel you mustn't forget.
What am I?

Answer: A swimming pool.

## Marni Lila Croft (7)
Etz Chaim Jewish Primary School, Mill Hill

# Play Time

It's green and red and orange in the
autumn.
The robins sing and eat their lunch at
the table.
The children play on the slide and swings.
The hens cluck and lay eggs for
our breakfast.
The fun continues with a bounce and flip.
The plants and trees sway in the wind
and rain.
The boys show their skills and shoot in
the net.
Daddy grows potatoes, carrots and leeks in
perfect lines.
This is my favourite place.
Where am I?

Answer: My garden.

## Annie Dolly Eva Sherman (7)
Etz Chaim Jewish Primary School, Mill Hill

# What Am I?

I am loud and busy in summer
And lots of fun.
I am wet and empty in winter,
I could do with some sun.
I can have some swings and slides.
If you're lucky I might have some rides.
You can go round the roundabout
And get dizzy
And sometimes I am very busy.
What am I?

Answer: A playground.

## Lily Roston (6)
Etz Chaim Jewish Primary School, Mill Hill

# Real Or Not?

I take something of yours
You no longer need
And leave money under your pillow.
I have beautiful, golden wings
That fluffer in the breeze.
I spread magical dust
But you will never see me
Because I only come while you are sleeping.
Who am I?

Answer: *The tooth fairy.*

**Libby Novick (7)**
Etz Chaim Jewish Primary School, Mill Hill

# Ticker

I have hands but I can't clap.
I have a face but I don't have a nose, mouth or eyes.
I tell but I don't speak.
I have numbers but I am not a ruler.
I move around but I have no legs.
I can tell you if you're early or late.
What am I?

Answer: A clock.

## Gabi Greenfield (7)
Etz Chaim Jewish Primary School, Mill Hill

# Chewing Tool

You are born with none.
As you grow so will they.
They wibble, wobble and come out.
A magical fairy comes
And collects them and leaves a coin.
You have more as an adult
Than as a child.
You brush them twice a day.
What are they?

Answer: Teeth.

## Annabelle Linton (6)

Etz Chaim Jewish Primary School, Mill Hill

# The Hairy Drum

I'm brown and hairy
And you may think I'm ugly,
But cut me open
And you will see I am white and shiny.
I have so many uses...
Eat me,
Drink me,
Make oil from me,
And you can even play me as a drum.
What am I?

Answer: A coconut.

## Jackson Sonny Novick (7)
Etz Chaim Jewish Primary School, Mill Hill

# A Special Treat

I feel like a soft pillow.
I have icing, sweets and sprinkles on top.
I taste delicious.
I'm sweet.
Sometimes, inside me there's jam
and cream.
People eat me at celebrations.
What am I?

Answer: A cake.

## Benji Daly (6)
Etz Chaim Jewish Primary School, Mill Hill

# Relaxing

I have lots of pages.
I have lots of words.
I have numbers on every page.
Pictures on me help you read.
There is a title on my front cover.
There is a blurb on my back cover.
What am I?

Answer: A book.

**Jamie Myers (6)**
Etz Chaim Jewish Primary School, Mill Hill

# It Gets Used A Lot

It is something that belongs to you
But other people use it more.
It has a capital letter.
You get it when you are a baby.
Everyone has one.
It is on your clothes.
What is it?

Answer: Your name.

## Sylvie Montefiore (6)
Etz Chaim Jewish Primary School, Mill Hill

# Writer

I have lots of small buttons.
Sometimes you play games on me.
You need to charge me.
I can be used in any place.
You can fold me.
You can use me to shop with.
What am I?

Answer: A computer.

## Eliana Sapphira Whiteman (6)
Etz Chaim Jewish Primary School, Mill Hill

# A Colourful Cocoon

I have the same shapes
On both sides of my body.
I fly every day.
I am very colourful.
I used to crawl like a worm.
I used to sleep in a colourful cocoon.
What am I?

Answer: A butterfly.

**Lexi Sliver (6)**
Etz Chaim Jewish Primary School, Mill Hill

# Night Mystery

I follow you everywhere.
I am bright and beautiful.
I am dark but give off light.
I am there but you can't always see me.
I can glow.
I can change shape.
What am I?

Answer: The moon.

## Ollie Lewis (7)
Etz Chaim Jewish Primary School, Mill Hill

# What Am I?

I sit in a cone.
I have lots of sprinkles.
I am cold.
I am sugary.
I am sweet.
I come in lots of flavours.
I mostly get eaten in the summer.
What am I?

Answer: Ice cream.

## Seth Shindler (7)
Etz Chaim Jewish Primary School, Mill Hill

# What Am I?

I'm the dino king with huge jaws,
Short arms and scary claws.
I have green skin that you can't beat
And small animals... I eat their meat!
What am I?

Answer: A T-rex.

## Teddy Jack Rose (6)
Etz Chaim Jewish Primary School, Mill Hill

# Snappy

I am green.
People think I am mean.
I have scales on my back.
I am always ready to attack.
I am a reptile.
I live in the Nile.
What am I?

Answer: A crocodile.

## Dalya Goldstone (7)
Etz Chaim Jewish Primary School, Mill Hill

# Monkey's Lunch

I grow on a tree.
I have dots on my peel.
I am tasty to eat.
I grow in hot countries.
Monkeys love to eat me.
I am yellow.
What am I?

Answer: A banana.

**Jayden Bentley (6)**
Etz Chaim Jewish Primary School, Mill Hill

# Spend, Spend, Spend

I have a tail.
I am made of metal.
If you drop me I will not break.
I have a head.
I am not a snake.
A bank has lots of me.
What am I?

Answer: A coin.

## Samuel Godfrey (6)
Etz Chaim Jewish Primary School, Mill Hill

# Building Materials

I am brown.
I dry quickly.
I am good at making buildings.
I am made in a mixer.
I am very useful.
I rhyme with lament.
What am I?

Answer: Cement.

## Ruby Carr (7)
Etz Chaim Jewish Primary School, Mill Hill

# Fluttering Colours

I fly in the sky.
I'm very colourful.
I'm very small.
I have got wings.
My baby has no wings.
What am I?

Answer: A butterfly.

## Jessica Lazarus (6)
Etz Chaim Jewish Primary School, Mill Hill

# Kick A Ball

I am round.
You kick me.
You play with me.
You can save me.
I am a name of a game.
I am hard.
What am I?

Answer: A football.

## Leo Rosenthal (6)
Etz Chaim Jewish Primary School, Mill Hill

# The Other Way Round

In the beginning, my name was the other way around.
It's in the summertime I can mainly be found.
I am born in the light of the bright sparkling moon
But change three times before I am doomed.
My clothes are made of the colours of rainbows
And patterned like beautiful, stained-glass windows.
Floating around, I display all my powers,
As I dance about between petals and flowers.
What am I?

Answer: A butterfly.

## Elysse Adil (7)
Grimsdell Mill Hill Pre-Preparatory School, Mill Hill

# Hairy Coconut

I have a hard shell but I am a mammal.
I feel like a coconut
But I don't grow on a tree.
I dig holes but I don't live in them.
I can sleep for 16 hours
And then I am awake.
I can smell very well
But I don't have good eyesight.
I don't like breakfast cereal
But I do like to eat insects.
What am I?

Answer: An armadillo.

## Saphira Vale-Harris (7)
Grimsdell Mill Hill Pre-Preparatory School, Mill Hill

# Lucky

I'm considered lucky in the Far East.
Turn me upside down
And I still remain the same.
I have my mates around me.
I'm only lonely once.
I'm made up of two rings,
One stacked on top of the other.
I rhyme with 'mate'.
Think octopus and planets
And you will know the answer.
What am I?

Answer: The number 8.

## Dylan Santangelo (5)
Grimsdell Mill Hill Pre-Preparatory School, Mill Hill

# Frozen Mountain

I am white and very large.
I can travel by water.
Polar bears can sometimes travel on me
And even the brave human explorers
have travelled on me.
If I travel too far I can become very small
and even disappear.
If I hit a ship I can sink it.
My name has to do with a mountain.
What am I?

Answer: An iceberg.

## Ekaterina Kasatkina (7)
Grimsdell Mill Hill Pre-Preparatory School, Mill Hill

# Ride The Wave

The wind in my hair.
The waves crashing like snow.
The salt in my mouth.
The sun reflecting like diamonds in the night sky.
The board as rough as the coral below.
The thrill of the chase.
The buzz of riding the wave.
What am I?

Answer: A surfer.

## Adam Coulstock (6)
Grimsdell Mill Hill Pre-Preparatory School, Mill Hill

# The Common Package

I have been around for more than 6,000 years.
I have multiple green or purple layers.
I can be long or round as a bouncy ball.
I can be crunchy or as soft as a pillow.
They like me as I contain lots of letter treasures.
What am I?

Answer: A cabbage.

## Ishan Vivek Mahan (6)

Grimsdell Mill Hill Pre-Preparatory School, Mill Hill

# A Graceful Swimmer

I have a flat body.
I glide through the water.
I have giant wings.
My tail is spiky
But does not sting.
Elegant and free, floating through the ocean,
That's the way to be!
What am I?

Answer: A giant manta ray.

## Jacob Courts (5)
Grimsdell Mill Hill Pre-Preparatory School, Mill Hill

# Stumped

I have a bark.
I wave in the wind.
I change my clothes every season.
I can make paper.
I can have many rings.
I am good for the environment.
I come in many shapes, sizes and colours.
What am I?

Answer: A tree.

## Jessica Jina (6)
Grimsdell Mill Hill Pre-Preparatory School, Mill Hill

# Around The North Pole

I live in the Arctic.
I hunt Arctic animals
Like seals, polar bears, walruses and
muskox.
I ride a sleigh pulled by huskies.
I throw meat for the huskies to eat.
I live near Santa Claus.
Who am I?

Answer: An Inuit.

## Penelope Derrer (7)

Grimsdell Mill Hill Pre-Preparatory School, Mill Hill

# What Am I?

The days are short
And the nights are long.
It is cold and wet
And sometimes it snows.
We stay inside
And drink hot chocolate.
If we are lucky,
We go outside and have a slide!
What is it?

Answer: Winter.

## Eden Protei (6)
Grimsdell Mill Hill Pre-Preparatory School, Mill Hill

# My Favourite Thing

I always make you smile.
I can be tall or short.
I can be light or dark.
I can be hot or cold.
I can be bitter or sweet.
I can help to wake you up,
Or put you to sleep.
What am I?

Answer: Chocolate milk.

## Skyler Stringer (6)

Grimsdell Mill Hill Pre-Preparatory School, Mill Hill

# What Am I?

I have black and white skin.
I have a pointed beak.
I have two wings but I can't fly.
I can do gymnastics in the sea.
I like eating fish and squid.
I live in a cold place.
What am I?

Answer: A penguin.

## Elizabeth Liu (5)
Grimsdell Mill Hill Pre-Preparatory School, Mill Hill

# What Am I?

I am a sphere.
I like to be on a pitch.
I like to be kicked into the goal.
I am a very hard sphere.
I like to be kicked really hard
And it doesn't hurt me.
What am I?

Answer: A football.

## Dani Pachon (6)
Grimsdell Mill Hill Pre-Preparatory School, Mill Hill

# Fire Power

Up, up, up and away I go
To travel to far away places.
I carry very special people.
I make them very happy
But to go inside me, don't forget your
nappy.
What am I?

Answer: A spaceship.

## Anthony Eden (6)
Grimsdell Mill Hill Pre-Preparatory School, Mill Hill

# Swimming Beauty

I live in the sea.
I have arms but no legs.
I have beautiful long hair.
I have a colourful tail.
You know me in books and movies
But nobody has seen me.
What am I?

Answer: A mermaid.

## Soha Jilani (5)
Grimsdell Mill Hill Pre-Preparatory School, Mill Hill

# What Am I?

I am round, black and white.
The boy kicks me with his left or right.
I score lots of goals in the back of the net.
Did I win the FA Cup?
Yes, you bet!
What am I?

Answer: A football.

## Jack Lever (6)
Grimsdell Mill Hill Pre-Preparatory School, Mill Hill

# Spiky

I have red eyes.
I have orange feet.
I like eating crabs.
I have a white belly.
I like to hop.
I have yellow and black, spiky feathers.
What am I?

Answer: A rockhopper penguin.

## Joshua Chu (5)
Grimsdell Mill Hill Pre-Preparatory School, Mill Hill

# Soles

I wear them every day.
They come in different sizes.
They come in pairs.
They come in many colours.
They have different styles.
I walk in them.
What are they?

*Answer: Shoes.*

## Sophia Waite (6)
Grimsdell Mill Hill Pre-Preparatory School, Mill Hill

# Fluffy Cutey

I'm cute and furry.
I eat carrots.
I love bouncing up and down.
I have very long ears.
I always bounce up the hills
And down the hills.
What am I?

Answer: A rabbit.

## Poppy Jenner (6)
Grimsdell Mill Hill Pre-Preparatory School, Mill Hill

# Snowy

I have black skin
And transparent fur.
I have 42 teeth.
I live in the Arctic.
I hunt for seals.
I am the biggest carnivore on land.
What am I?

Answer: A polar bear.

## Rayan Valoti (6)
Grimsdell Mill Hill Pre-Preparatory School, Mill Hill

# What Am I?

I eat fish.
I am good at swimming.
I lay eggs.
I cannot fly but I can flap.
I have oil on me.
I am black and white.
I have feet.
What am I?

Answer: A penguin.

## Ela Yilmaz (6)
Grimsdell Mill Hill Pre-Preparatory School, Mill Hill

# Running Lightning

He is as quick as lightning.
He has the power of lightning.
He is a superhero in DC.
He has lived in the Speed Force.
His skin is red.
Who is he?

Answer: The Flash.

## Artin Edalatian (6)
Grimsdell Mill Hill Pre-Preparatory School, Mill Hill

# Let's Fly!

I can be built.
I can fly.
I have a string.
You can run with me.
I come in different colours.
I come in different shapes and sizes.
What am I?

Answer: A kite.

## Evie Pincherle (7)
Grimsdell Mill Hill Pre-Preparatory School, Mill Hill

# Big And Juicy

I am healthy and I'm sweet.
I am a real treat to eat.
I have seeds all over me.
I am very good to see.
I am red all over.
What am I?

Answer: A strawberry.

## Jessica Fridman (6)
Grimsdell Mill Hill Pre-Preparatory School, Mill Hill

# Toytastic!

I am made of bricks.
I have hands but no fingers.
I am a film star.
I have many guises.
There are more of me than humans.
Who am I?

*Answer: Lego Man.*

## James Sansome (6)
Grimsdell Mill Hill Pre-Preparatory School, Mill Hill

# Fly In The Sky

I can fly in the sky.
I have colourful wings
And black antennae.
I like flowers
And I come out in the sunshine.
What am I?

Answer: A butterfly.

## Layla Mia Sakerchand (5)
Grimsdell Mill Hill Pre-Preparatory School, Mill Hill

# In The Jungle

I am spotty.
I eat meat.
I have sharp teeth.
I can climb trees.
I live in the rainforest.
I am camouflaged.
What am I?

Answer: A Jaguar.

## Uma Dhanak (6)
Grimsdell Mill Hill Pre-Preparatory School, Mill Hill

# Waddle

I have an orange beak.
I can't fly but I can swim.
My favourite food is fish.
I live in the South Pole.
What am I?

Answer: A penguin.

## Oyku Ada Istanbullu (6)
Grimsdell Mill Hill Pre-Preparatory School, Mill Hill

# The Cool Song

I am as white as snow.
I am as soft as wool.
I live in the Arctic.
People think I am very cool.
What am I?

Answer: A polar bear.

## Shloka Chheda-Varma (7)
Grimsdell Mill Hill Pre-Preparatory School, Mill Hill

# What Am I?

I am fluffy.
I look like a rainbow.
I have a pointy, magic horn.
I look cute.
What am I?

Answer: A unicorn.

**Maria Votinova (6)**
Grimsdell Mill Hill Pre-Preparatory School, Mill Hill

# The Tallest Animal

My height is helpful for keeping
a lookout for predators.
I'm a herbivore and only eat plants
like the sweet acacia tree.
I am a very social animal
and roam around in groups.
I live in Africa and normally inhabit
savannahs and woodlands.
I have very long legs
and I have a pattern on my back.
I have a ginormous, long tongue.
What am I?

Answer: A giraffe.

## Isabella Clifford (6)

Rimon Jewish Primary School, Golders Green

# Zoom, Zoom

I'm made of metal and a bit of glass.
I take-off really, really fast.
I take you away and I have big wings.
You can eat yummy food and buy lots
of things.
There are buttons at the front you must
not press.
Behave yourself, don't make a mess!
What am I?

Answer: An aeroplane.

## Zac Reuben (7)
Rimon Jewish Primary School, Golders Green

# Goal!

I am black and white.
I am quite light.
My shape is round.
I spin on the ground.
Give me a kick
But don't give me a lick.
I can be passed to a friend
Until the game ends.
When the whistle blows,
My team goes.
What am I?

Answer: A football.

## Max Silverman (6)
Rimon Jewish Primary School, Golders Green

# Off We Go!

You sit in me to go to a different place.
Sometimes I can be in a race.
I'm either red, black, blue, green or white
And I turn my lights on at night!
Sometimes I am electric, sometimes not.
I open my top when it is hot!
What am I?

Answer: A car.

## Emilie Vertes (7)

Rimon Jewish Primary School, Golders Green

# At A Shop

You can draw with me.
I can come in lots of colours.
I can be big or small.
You can get me from most shops.
I can draw a building's map.
Teachers might use me a lot.
I sometimes run out of ink.
What am I?

Answer: A pen.

## Sammy Belnikoff (7)
Rimon Jewish Primary School, Golders Green

# Kick Me

Please kick me,
Please kick me.
I can go right in the goal.
The goalkeeper won't save me
Because I'm so hard and bold.
I will go through his legs
And right in the goal.
What am I?

Answer: A ball.

## Zeph Quint (6)
Rimon Jewish Primary School, Golders Green

# Safety

My favourite colour is yellow.
I work on the street.
I work with zebras and pelicans.
I am very careful.
Like a superhero, I stop cars.
Some people think I taste nice.
What am I?

Answer: A lollipop lady.

**Eliana Barasi (7)**
Rimon Jewish Primary School, Golders Green

# What Am I?

I have a red car.
I wear a helmet.
I use my siren's sound for an emergency.
I have a ladder on my truck.
I am very brave and extraordinary.
I save people.
What am I?

Answer: A fireman.

## Mylee Victoria White (7)
Rimon Jewish Primary School, Golders Green

# I Am Fierce

I am poisonous.
I am dangerous.
I am fierce.
I am a reptile.
I am a carnivore.
I am real but I am called
by the name of a legendary creature.
What am I?

Answer: A Komodo dragon.

## Julia Movshovitz (6)
Rimon Jewish Primary School, Golders Green

# Winter

I am cold.
Sometimes I wear a scarf.
You build me outside.
It is fun to build me.
You could eat my nose.
I will be gone when spring comes.
What am I?

Answer: A snowman.

## Lila Barasi (5)
Rimon Jewish Primary School, Golders Green

# Light And Crafty

I come from a tree up high,
If you fold me, I might even fly.
You can cut me up,
Colour me in,
Roll me up and I am very thin.
What am I?

Answer: Paper.

## Lily Greenfeld (6)
Rimon Jewish Primary School, Golders Green

# Joy And Fun

A little bit of rain, a little bit of sun,
The sudden rainbow that glows beautifully
in the sky.
The grass grows and flowers bloom.
The sounds of children playing
And laughing outdoors.
Everywhere is pretty, everyone is happy.
Even the animals skip
And race through the fields.
What am I?

Answer: Spring.

## Candre Chukwuemeka (7)
St James CE Primary School, Northampton

# Squeak!

I am an animal.
I am petite.
I am soft.
I come in different colours.
I am furry.
I can squeak.
I am very shy.
What am I?

Answer: A mouse.

## Abbie Radu (7)
St James CE Primary School, Northampton

# The Sea Terror

I live under the ocean.
I eat kelp.
Sometimes I wash up on a shore.
I am as spiky as a sledgehammer
covered in thorns.
I am as round as the ball David
Beckham kicks.
To get my spikes out you have
to use vinegar.
What am I?

Answer: A sea urchin.

## Darwin Kafka (7)
St Mark's CE Primary School, Islington

# Colourful World

It smells like a chocolate ice cream that is
very yummy.
It is as squishy as a teddy.
It is a colourful place and smells good.
It can have a water bottle, bag and a teddy.
It can smell really nice.
It can have squishy Play-Doh.
What is it?

Answer: Smiggle.

## Amy Bala (7)
St Mark's CE Primary School, Islington

# What Am I?

I'm a fierce, strong carnivore.
I live in the dark, scary jungle.
I'm as strong as a grey rock.
My bones are as giant as a stone.
I have yellow, furry hair.
My roar is as loud as the giant wind.
What am I?

Answer: A lion.

## Joel Tesfamariam (7)
St Mark's CE Primary School, Islington

# Runner

I like running as fast as Usain Bolt.
I am as stripy as a zebra crossing.
I have whiskers as scary as a ghost.
I am a carnivore, I love eating meat.
I am a cat, a big cat.
I am as creepy as a pirate.
What am I?

Answer: A tiger.

## Joshua Daynes (6)
St Mark's CE Primary School, Islington

# Milk-Drinker

I drink milk from my mum.
I'm as cute as a baby.
I'm as furry as a hairball.
I lie on top of hot spots on cars.
Everybody thinks I'm cute.
I have black and white fur
And whiskers.
What am I?

Answer: A kitten.

## Inka Druszcz (7)
St Mark's CE Primary School, Islington

# The Milk-Liker

I walk like a horse
When I break my paw.
I am as ginger as ginger hair.
I am as fussy as a bunny.
I have claws as sharp as a knife.
I have soft paws like a pillow.
I like cotton balls and milk.
What am I?

Answer: A cat.

## Tia Kallaste Akesen (6)
St Mark's CE Primary School, Islington

# What Is It?

Its tail is as red as a chilli.
It's very big like a giraffe.
It lives in a dark and spooky cave.
It's very scary.
It's red like a red rabbit.
It breathes fire.
What is it?

Answer: A dragon.

## Ruby Parkhurst (6)
St Mark's CE Primary School, Islington

# Shine Colourfully

It is colourful and cute.
You might have bought some things from there.
It has pens.
It has lots of colours.
You might want to visit.
I have things from there.
What is it?

Answer: Smiggle.

## Layla Cole (7)
St Mark's CE Primary School, Islington

# The School-Taker

I am any colour.
You can take me anywhere.
I am good for carrying.
You can put stuff in me.
You mostly take me to school.
You wear me on your back.
What am I?

Answer: A backpack.

**Poppy Haigh (7)**
St Mark's CE Primary School, Islington

# Cute Prowler

I have sharp claws.
I drink white, freezing milk.
I am as cute as a pet mouse.
I am in an animal family.
I have four short legs.
I have a swishing tail.
What am I?

Answer: A cat.

## Yerim Baek (6)
St Mark's CE Primary School, Islington

# The Wild Animal

I'm as wild as a storm.
I'm a mammal.
I am a hairy animal.
I'm a big cat.
I eat meat.
I'm the king of the jungle.
What am I?

Answer: A lion.

## Grace (7)
St Mark's CE Primary School, Islington

# What Am I?

I look like a person
And I live in the sea.
I like playing with my dolphin friend.
I have scales on my tail.
I'm a lovely girl.
What am I?

Answer: A mermaid.

## Yohana Yonata (5)
St Mark's CE Primary School, Islington

# Sneaker

I have four legs.
I am not stripy.
I am yellow.
I am wild.
I hunt overnight.
My baby is called a cub.
I have a mane.
What am I?

Answer: A lion.

## Nahom Yonata (7)
St Mark's CE Primary School, Islington

# The Insects That Are Nice

I am pretty on every side.
Every day, I fly in the sky.
I am scared if people move
When I am on them.
I love flowers.
What am I?

Answer: A butterfly.

## Cerys Rosel Miller (5)
St Mark's CE Primary School, Islington

# Secret Birds

I have two wings.
I like jewellery.
I am black and white.
I have two legs.
I have a beak.
I have hair on my body.
What am I?

Answer: A magpie.

## Olive Boyd (5)
St Mark's CE Primary School, Islington

# Mr White

I look like a ball of wool.
I am warm.
I eat grass.
I have four legs.
I make a 'baa' noise.
What am I?

Answer: A sheep.

## Malik Adam (6)
St Mark's CE Primary School, Islington

# The Magic Collector

I have little wings.
I have a crown.
I like teeth.
I can fly in the sky.
I am little.
What am I?

Answer: The Tooth Fairy.

## Mae English (5)
St Mark's CE Primary School, Islington

# The Secret Animal

I am green.
I can camouflage.
I eat flies.
I sneak up on my prey.
I hide from predators.
What am I?

Answer: A chameleon.

## Alistair Turner (6)
St Mark's CE Primary School, Islington

# Friendly Fish

It eats smelly fish.
It likes to jump in the water.
It makes a happy sound.
What is it?

Answer: A dolphin.

## Alicia Chin (5)
St Mark's CE Primary School, Islington

# What Am I?

I look like a fleece
And I am orange.
I have four legs.
I am bad.
What am I?

Answer: A lion.

## George Pipinka (6)
St Mark's CE Primary School, Islington

# What Am I?

I have four legs.
I can run on grass.
I can run very fast.
What am I?

Answer: A cheetah.

## Shiloh Daley (5)
St Mark's CE Primary School, Islington

# Crawling Everywhere

I am on my hands and knees.
When I get tired I have a nap.
When I wake up I sit on my mum's lap.
Milk is sweet, lovely and soothing.
I look at the world and it's always moving.
One day I'll know a lot of things about the world.
I'll travel the globe to the dry plains of Africa.
When I get home I'll tell my mum I've been to Rome and Africa
To see the creatures.
What am I?

Answer: A baby.

## Faith Leslie Smith (7)
St Martin's School, Mill Hill

# Popular Brown

I am rectangular and have squares in me.
I am thin like a notebook.
I am always wrapped in a shiny dress.
Under my dress, I am brown and naked.
If you hold me tight I am going to melt.
I am popular so everyone likes me a lot.
I am yummy and I can make you happy.
What am I?

Answer: Chocolate.

## Jin Kobayashi (6)
St Martin's School, Mill Hill

# Bounce

I can be soft or hard.
I come in different sizes.
I come in different colours.
If you throw me I won't break.
If you kick me it will not hurt me.
Boys, girls and adults love to play with me.
What am I?

Answer: A ball.

## Bami Disu (6)
St Martin's School, Mill Hill

# A View From Above

Sometimes I can cause trouble.
I like to look down at people.
I have a beak but no teeth.
I make a nest above the ground.
I lay eggs.
I like to eat worms.
I have wings.
I can fly.
What am I?

Answer: A bird.

## Michael Burgess (7)
St Martin's School, Mill Hill

# Huge And Green

I am really red and sweet,
Green from outside, black in seed,
Like a melon but full of water.
My slices are lovely indeed,
In a fruit salad or even alone,
I am delicious after a feed.
What am I?

Answer: A watermelon.

## Dylan Attar (7)
St Martin's School, Mill Hill

# Flying In The Air

I can go on water, land
And in the air.
I am big and noisy.
I can take you anywhere.
I have many different names.
People can walk in me.
My skin is as hard as a rock.
What am I?

Answer: An aeroplane.

## Max Ng (7)
St Martin's School, Mill Hill

# One Of A Kind!

I look a little odd like Frankenstein.
All different parts make my body.
I come from down under.
Flat-footed, beak, tail, fur.
I swim like a fish.
What am I?

Answer: A platypus.

## Peter De Souza-Feighoney (6)
St Martin's School, Mill Hill

# In The Garden

I fly.
I am a bug.
I have red wings.
I have black spots.
I have a black skin.
I live in the garden.
What am I?

Answer: A ladybird.

## Alan Jalal (6)
St Martin's School, Mill Hill

# School Rider

I am a metallic kind of material.
I have a comfy seat.
I have a bell that goes *ting, ting.*
You can ride on me at any time
Or if you want to go to school.
You can paint me any colour or pattern.
I can go very fast and quick.
What am I?

Answer: A bike.

## Emilio Mataj (7)
Starks Field Primary School, Edmonton

# The African Hunter

I have a big furry face.
I roar like the wind, blowing trees
And houses down.
I like to hide in the long grass, hunting
And sniffing my prey.
I like living in Africa with my wild friends
Or you might find me at the zoo.
What am I?

Answer: A lion.

## Ruby May Penn (6)
Starks Field Primary School, Edmonton

# The Changing Stick

I look like a brown stick but I move around.
I have eight legs that look like tiny sticks.
I am skinny like a stick.
I change to a stick when I am scared.
Sometimes I have green leaves on me.
I walk on brown trees.
What am I?

Answer: A stick insect.

## Halima Said (6)
Starks Field Primary School, Edmonton

# The Dangerous Hunter

I have green scales that are bumpy.
I have sharp, white, scary, pointy teeth.
I am a green, dangerous, living dinosaur.
I am wider than a tree.
I have white, sharp claws.
I like to eat people that are delicious.
What am I?

Answer: A crocodile.

## Stefano Brusa (6)
Starks Field Primary School, Edmonton

# Galloping Animal

I have four, furry, thin legs
And two shiny, ginger ears.
You can ride on me
But I am not a horse.
I don't like to be stroked by strangers.
I have a long, ginger tail that wiggles.
I have blue eyes.
What am I?

Answer: A donkey.

## Ellie Louise Richards (7)
Starks Field Primary School, Edmonton

# Helping Hand

I help people every day.
I wear a hat black or blue.
If you're naughty, I'll take you away.
If you're lost I'll help you find your way.
I help the traffic every day.
I make the rules.
What am I?

Answer: A policeman.

## Ameera Haque (7)
Starks Field Primary School, Edmonton

# Crunch, Crunch

I am different colours.
In autumn I fall down.
I'm on the top of the tree.
I'm on the floor
And make crunching sounds.
I blow in the wind.
I am sometimes in bushes hiding.
What am I?

Answer: A leaf.

## Jeremiah Chinonso Nwoke (6)
Starks Field Primary School, Edmonton

# High Jumper

I can jump side to side.
I have furry, brown, soft skin.
I can never stop jumping.
I always hop like a green frog.
I run like a fast cat.
I eat lots of delicious carrots.
What am I?

Answer: A bunny.

## Aisling Dorcas Adejori (6)
Starks Field Primary School, Edmonton

# What Am I?

I jump like a kangaroo.
I eat a healthy snack.
You can find me in a campsite.
I am fluffy with a pom-pom tail.
You might spot me in a garden.
I live in a deep hole.
What am I?

Answer: A bunny.

## Lily-Rose Cruickshank (7)
Starks Field Primary School, Edmonton

# Jumping Around

I jump like a cat
But I'm not a cat.
I am as white as the snow.
I eat green grass.
I have four jumpy legs.
I have two floppy ears.
I have a pink nose.
What am I?

Answer: A rabbit.

## Gabriela Ivaylova Ivanova (7)
Starks Field Primary School, Edmonton

# What Am I?

I wear a special uniform.
I can run fast like the wind.
My car has a siren on the top.
I carry a taser.
I have a walkie-talkie.
I keep people safe.
What am I?

Answer: A policeman.

## Christian Kardzhaliyski (7)
Starks Field Primary School, Edmonton

# A Healthy Hand

I have vitamin C.
I can be sweet or sour.
I have orange skin.
You peel me.
On the inside I am squishy.
I grow from a tiny seed.
What am I?

Answer: An orange.

## Mehnaz Alam (7)
Starks Field Primary School, Edmonton

# Mr Fluffy

I have hard, black eyes.
I am colourful.
I am cute.
I am not alive.
Children love to hug me.
I cannot breathe.
What am I?

Answer: A teddy.

## Ediz Jeysan Ibrahim (7)
Starks Field Primary School, Edmonton

# My Favourite Fruit

I am really juicy and red.
When you have a big, crunchy bite
Juice squirts out!
I have a green leaf when I fall from the tree.
You can buy me from the shops
And you must wash me before you eat me.
What am I?

Answer: An apple.

## Abigail Jenny Ochan (7)
The Willow Primary School, Tottenham

# Roar!

I have sharp claws.
I have hair around my face.
My tail is long.
I have a big, furry mane.
I roam the African wild.
I hunt for my prey.
I have a fierce roar.
I am the king of the jungle.
What am I?

Answer: A lion.

## Renaé Beckford (7)
The Willow Primary School, Tottenham

# Poison Monster

I camouflage in the great, green grass.
If you want to survive, run and hide.
If you're not accurate you will die!
I slither, I am poisonous and bite.
Watch that eye, you don't want to die!
What am I?

Answer: A snake.

## Abdulrahman Rage (7)
The Willow Primary School, Tottenham

# Black Mystery

It's dark.
It's up high.
There's a rocket.
You can't see a thing.
What's that round thing?
What are those tiny things up there?
Where is it?

*Answer: Space.*

## Solomon Goddard-Banks (6)
The Willow Primary School, Tottenham

# People Carrier

I can go fast
And I can play music.
I have wheels to make it go fast.
I am red.
I have a sign at the front of me
And the back of me.
What am I?

Answer: A car.

## Natasha Anakaye Stevens (7)
The Willow Primary School, Tottenham

# What Am I?

I am furry.
You can cuddle me.
I have fluffy hair.
I have a fierce roar.
I'm the king of the jungle.
I hunt for prey.
What am I?

Answer: A lion.

## Luis Ciku (7)

The Willow Primary School, Tottenham

# My Fruit

I am yellow and I have a brown bit.
I am something healthy to eat.
I have a curved shape.
I have no fur but I have yellow skin.
What am I?

Answer: A banana.

## Ilhan Musah (7)
The Willow Primary School, Tottenham

# Wheel Power

It has got a red roof.
It has powerful wheels.
It runs on tracks.
Lots of people can sit inside.
It has lots of windows.
What is it?

Answer: A train.

## Ike Lemeh (7)
The Willow Primary School, Tottenham

# What Am I?

I stand still.
I am made out of wood.
I am tall.
I have branches.
I have leaves.
I eat energy from the sun.
What am I?

Answer: A tree.

## Nadirah Nasir (7)
The Willow Primary School, Tottenham

# What Vehicle Am I?

I have one wheel.
I am a bit wobbly,
I'm easy to fall off.
You sometimes see clowns riding on me.
What am I?

Answer: A unicycle.

## Mert Tintas (6)
The Willow Primary School, Tottenham

# Zoomer

I am long.
I am fast.
I go on tracks.
I even go underground.
I have edges and windows.
What am I?

Answer: A train.

## Prince Auguste (6)
The Willow Primary School, Tottenham

# Stripy Herbivore

I have stripes.
I am soft.
I have a short tail.
I am a herbivore.
I eat grass.
What am I?

Answer: A zebra.

## Jayden Taylor-Macauley (6)
The Willow Primary School, Tottenham

# Fast Vehicle

I am big.
I can go fast in the city.
I am amazing.
People drive me.
What am I?

Answer: A car.

## Patrick Mpanumpanu (7)
The Willow Primary School, Tottenham

# Wonderful Wings

It flies backwards
And forwards when it has wings.
It lashes out with its tongue at everything.
It goes very fast.
It changes colour.
It eats bugs and flies.
It likes to whizz around.
It is an invertebrate.
It is cold-blooded.
It has wonderful wings.
It has fast wings.
What is it?

Answer: A dragonfly.

## Chukwuma Okongwu (5)
UCS Pre-Prep, London

# Birds

They can fly
But they can't say hi or bye!
They're as cute, jolly
And tiny as a monkey.
At night they're always right!
They are cute but not mute.
They can sing
But they have one chance of being king.
They are beautiful and can be colourful
What are they?

Answer: Birds.

## Sammy Kohansky (6)
UCS Pre-Prep, London

# What Is It?

It has didgeridoos
And kangaroos in the zoo.
It's as hot as a frying pan.
It's on the other side of the world.
It has the biggest rock in the world.
It's next to New Zealand.
They play Aussie Rules.
What is it?

Answer: Australia.

## Theo Postgate (5)
UCS Pre-Prep, London

# Fire

I am a fiery ball.
I am the biggest star of all.
I am the hottest star of all.
I am as hot as America
Solar storms cause the Northern Lights
And when they come everybody has fun
And eats buns.
What am I?

Answer: The sun.

## Freddie Harris (6)
UCS Pre-Prep, London

# What Am I?

I eat you.
If you come near me I will scratch
And catch you.
I am as strong as a building.
I am as fluffy as a bear.
I am a predator.
I am faster than you.
I can jump higher than you.
What am I?

*Answer: A tiger.*

## Gabriel Susskind (6)
UCS Pre-Prep, London

# Abyss

I have big flappy fins on my head.
I do not go to bed.
I spend my life hunting for worms
at the bottom of the sea.
When there are sixgill sharks around,
I propel myself upwards.
What am I?

Answer: A flapjack octopus.

**William Lacey (6)**
UCS Pre-Prep, London

# Scrummy Treat

I am yummy and scrummy.
I am full of Smarties.
I smell delicious.
Most people love me.
I am full of rainbows that shine.
I am great for parties.
I shout, "Happy birthday."
What am I?

Answer: A cake.

## Leah Livingstone (6)
UCS Pre-Prep, London

# Yummy

I am colourful.
You can eat me.
I am scrummy.
I am a cylinder shape.
Children love me
And I love it.
I have food colouring.
Lots of people eat me.
I am delicious.
What am I?

Answer: A rainbow cake.

**Toby Allen (6)**
UCS Pre-Prep, London

# What Am I?

How old am I?
I am six.
As hot as Israel
And the Maldives.
As great a footballer as Messi.
As weak as a worm.
As fast as Messi.
As terrifying as a tiger.
What am I?

*Answer: A football player.*

## Zac Collis (6)
UCS Pre-Prep, London

# Savannah Animal

I am very skinny.
I am very crafty.
I am a very small creature.
Giraffes step on me.
I clean lions' teeth.
I am very dirty
When I come out of his mouth.
What am I?

Answer: A lizard.

## Feyi Animashaun (6)
UCS Pre-Prep, London

# What Am I?

*Crash, bang* I go.
I am straight.
I am sharp.
I am used in battle.
Terrible sights of dead men.
*Boom, crash* go cannons.
The battle is won.
What am I?

Answer: A sword.

## Max Tager (5)
UCS Pre-Prep, London

# What Am I?

I have powerful, useful pads.
I have cool styles of me.
I have three cool fins.
I am so strong and tough.
I am fast and cool.
I am mighty and strong.
What am I?

Answer: A fidget spinner.

**Jacob Lee (5)**
UCS Pre-Prep, London

# What Am I?

I have lots of shiny things.
I'm the one that looks ahead.
I have shiny blue feathers
And some yellow.
I can be a pet.
I can copy what you say.
What am I?

Answer: A parrot.

## Adrian Bucher (5)
UCS Pre-Prep, London

# What Am I?

I go fast.
I go *vroom*.
I go *zoom*.
I have a shield with a bull
And a ring on the bull's head.
I am mainly white.
What am I?

Answer: A Lamborghini.

**Enitan Ajeigbe (6)**
UCS Pre-Prep, London

# What Am I?

I can't fly.
You can use me to snack!
You can eat me.
I have apples.
I can sit on the floor.
I have eight legs.
What am I?

Answer: An eight-legged apple person.

## Eric Wang (6)
UCS Pre-Prep, London

# What Am I?

Sometimes I am angry
And it makes me smelly!
I am black
And I like a snack!
I live in the hot desert
And I live in a burrow.
What am I?

Answer: A skunk.

## Kabir Jai Bordoloi (5)
UCS Pre-Prep, London

# King

It has black stripes.
It has powerful paws.
It is as strong as a car.
It has a tail.
It has pointy ears.
It likes to swim.
What is it?

Answer: A tiger.

## Ethan Shaw (5)
UCS Pre-Prep, London

# Swim, Deep Beach

I can be found on the beach
But not in the sea!
I fly but may not climb.
I say, "Squawk!"
But may not talk.
What am I?

Answer: A parrot.

## Sacha Livingstone (6)
UCS Pre-Prep, London

# Woof

I say *woof, bark, bark, bark!*
I sniff and scratch.
I say, "Give me a bone
And I'll eat it whole!"
What am I?

Answer: A puppy.

## Leo San (6)
UCS Pre-Prep, London

# What Am I?

I have long ears.
I have a pink nose.
Dogs sniff me out.
Dogs chase me.
Dogs pounce at me.
I like carrots.
What am I?

Answer: A rabbit.

## Emily Pratt (5)
UCS Pre-Prep, London

# What Am I?

I am soft and yummy
And I have chocolate.
I am big, delicious and good.
I am not healthy.
I am a food.
What am I?

Answer: A brownie.

## Even Chaitowitz (6)
UCS Pre-Prep, London

# What Am I?

I can fly.
I can talk.
I can walk.
I am a person's best friend.
I have colours.
I can sit.
What am I?

Answer: A parrot.

**Baer Bolton Smith (5)**
UCS Pre-Prep, London

# Yellow Cat

I am big and furry.
I am the king.
I live in India.
I eat zebras.
I am fast.
I eat cheetahs.
Who am I?

Answer: A lion.

## Avyan Kapur (5)
UCS Pre-Prep, London

# Who Is He?

He can talk.
He can walk.
He is stinky and smelly.
He can be naughty.
He wears boots.
Who is he?

Answer: My brother, Max.

## Sasha Steele (5)
UCS Pre-Prep, London

# What Am I?

I can make a buzzing sound.
I make a 'zzz' noise.
I am fast at flying.
What am I?

Answer: A dragonfly.

## Reuben Jerman-Lipus (5)
UCS Pre-Prep, London

# What Is It?

It has good players.
It is the best team.
It has the best vest.
What is it?

Answer: The Wolverhampton Wanderers.

## Amit Kumar (6)
UCS Pre-Prep, London

# In Space

It is in space.
Its home is in the galaxy.
It has you.
You need air.
What is it?

*Answer: The Earth.*

## Max San (6)
UCS Pre-Prep, London

# What Am I?

I am fluffy.
I am noisy.
I am sweet.
I have a tail.
I am pretty.
What am I?

Answer: A bunny.

## Lily Grace Nyman (6)
UCS Pre-Prep, London

# Who Am I?

I have a bow and arrow.
I am not green.
I am a boy.
I am white.
Who am I?

Answer: Robin Hood.

## Alfie Boujo (5)
UCS Pre-Prep, London

# I Am Unique!

I have jewels hidden in my house
But not in a case.
I make some rules
And sometimes give handy tools.
My birthday is in June
Of course, it's when I was due.
I am important and very unique.
I am in charge of everybody's seat.
If the police can't solve a crime,
I will find them like Optimus Prime.
Who am I?

Answer: The Queen.

## Marie Allali (7)
Wessex Gardens Primary School, Golders Green

# Spot My Colour And You Will Know

I come in all shapes and sizes,
Styles and colours.
You can ride me for miles and miles
But you can't use technology.
You have to use your body.
What am I?

Answer: A rainbow bicycle.

## Hassan Alaa (6)
Wessex Gardens Primary School, Golders Green

# Neat And Clean

I have many legs
But cannot stand.
I have a long neck
But no head.
I cannot see
And I am neat
And as tidy
As can be.
What am I?

Answer: A brush.

## Kinjal Rawat (7)
Wessex Gardens Primary School, Golders Green

# Tiger

I am fast.
I am strong.
I look sweet and cuddly
But I am very dangerous.
Don't cross my path,
I might bite.
What am I?

Answer: A tiger.

## Ilhan Coskum (6)
Wessex Gardens Primary School, Golders Green

# What Is It?

It's stretchy
And it's fun to play with it.
You can also make a bubble with it
But I like to play with it.
What is it?

Answer: Slime.

## Ali Aldahhan (6)
Wessex Gardens Primary School, Golders Green